This Book Belongs to:

_____

_____

Thanks for your purchase!
We hope you enjoy this Journal.
If you consider this notebook
useful please leave a review.

Thanks for your support.
You are Awesome!

www.ingramcontent.com/pod-product-compliance
Lightning Source LLC
LaVergne TN
LVHW082336130125
801208LV00036B/1006